NARROWBOAT CHEF'S

Winter Warmers

COLLECTION

First published in the UK in 2020 by Narrowboat Chef
www.narrowboatchef.com
books@narrowboatchef.com

ISBN: 978-1-8382941-0-6 (print)
ISBN: 978-1-8382941-1-3 (ebook)

Cover design by Margaret Duncan
Book design by Margaret Duncan
Food and canal photography by Margaret Duncan & Ryan Duncan
Back cover and family portrait photography by Stephen Williams
Edited by Twyla Akhurst

Dedication

This book is dedicated to everyone who has followed our adventure aboard our narrowboat – whether you've been with us from the start or just joined us recently. Thank you for your support and encouragement!

Contents

Introduction

Two and a half years ago, we moved from a one-bedroom apartment in the midlands of the UK to a 60-foot long, 7-foot wide narrowboat.

Yes, it's like living in a long hallway. Yes, you do have to get creative with storage. And no, it's actually *not* freezing in winter, thanks to our solid-fuel stove!

Who are we?

In case you aren't familiar with us, let us introduce ourselves; we are Maggie, Ryan, and Pixel the fox terrier. Apart from the dog, who was adopted here in the UK, we are Australians who moved to the UK almost six years ago, chasing our own adventure. We had chef qualifications under our belts, a small cushion of funds to keep us going for a few months, and lots of plans for our future on the other side of the world.

Pixel keeping warm by the fire.

 2

Our main goal in coming to the UK was to travel. We both love experiencing different cultures, trying exotic foods, and making new friends, and we especially wanted to see more of the country our ancestors came from. Considering Australia is a 28-hour flight away, it seemed the smart thing to move here permanently!

We were young, had no major debts, and no kids to worry about, so we figured why not? In fact, the hardest part of moving was getting Maggie's visa. After some initial setbacks, it was eventually approved and we hopped on a plane, arriving in London on Christmas Day, 2014.

Unfortunately, the dream didn't match reality...

We found it difficult to find the time to travel while both working full time as chefs, and also more expensive than we could reasonably afford after paying our bills. After two years, we started looking at alternative lifestyles that could give us more of what we were looking for.

Maggie steering a hire boat into a lock.

We stumbled across the idea of living on a narrowboat as a potential lifestyle option after Maggie's parents invited us to join them on a two-week narrowboat holiday. (We suspect the invitation was primarily extended so that they would have lackeys to do all the locks for them as we cruised a network of canals known as the Four Counties Ring.)

Honestly, at the end of that trip we were convinced that a narrowboat would *not* be the answer we were looking for. For one thing, steering a boat and doing locks is a lot of work and neither of us were particularly fit.

There were also our jobs to consider – ideally, we didn't want to be tied to a location-based job if we were to live on board a boat, but we weren't quite at the stage of working for ourselves or working online.

And speaking of internet, was it even *possible* for us to get internet on a boat!?

Finding a new dream

After some research, we gradually warmed to the idea of living on a narrowboat. Turns out, you can get internet on a boat!

In February of 2018 we bought our second-hand narrowboat, *Andrea Rose*. She's a wonderful narrowboat with everything we need on board. We moved aboard that March and began the process of setting ourselves up to continuously cruise the 2,000 miles of canal network.

We finally had everything in place in November 2018 and started cruising full time. We also started our YouTube channel, Narrowboat Chef, that same month. We wanted to document our adventure for our families back home in Australia, for ourselves to look back on, and also for any others who might find our videos entertaining.

We also figured it would be a great opportunity to share cooking tips and recipes from our days as chefs and demonstrate that it's not hard to make restaurant-quality meals in your own home. Even if your kitchen is a small galley on a small boat!

Since then, we've been sharing our cruising journeys, recipes, and explorations of the surrounding English countryside with our followers on YouTube and we've loved every minute of it! We've had breakdowns (engine ones, not mental ones!), we've been stuck in locks, we've redecorated, we've even had our engine completely pulled out of the boat! We've seen and done so much more than we would have if we'd stayed in that apartment. And it's only been two and a half years!

Operating a lock on the Trent and Mersey Canal in Staffordshire.

Pixel helping with the food photography!

Writing this cookbook

If you've been following us for a while, you'll know that this cookbook was originally set to be released a year ago in November of 2019... Obviously, that didn't happen. No specific reason other than we didn't plan very well and the overwhelming nature of the project got to us. Writing a cookbook is no simple task!

As with all of our recipes on our Narrowboat Chef channel, the recipes in this book are designed to be as simple and straight-forward as possible. Cooking delicious food shouldn't be hard and we try to show that. We've also cooked each and every one in our galley kitchen – so if we can manage in our small kitchen, you can too!

Being tucked away on a cozy narrowboat enjoying the aroma of a stew as it bubbles on top of the solid-fuel stove is a little piece of heaven. With this idea in mind, the theme of this cookbook is warm and hearty recipes that are perfect for the crisp autumn days and dark winter nights that we in the northern hemisphere experience during the last months of one year and the first months of the next. Definitely very different to the summer Christmases we experienced in Australia!

We hope you'll find a new favourite recipe among the pages of this book. We've also included photos of our autumnal adventures on the canals and frosted mornings in our winter marina that we hope you'll enjoy.

Maggie, Ryan & Pixel

Narrowboat Chef Channel ▶

@NarrowboatChef 🐦

@NarrowboatChef f

@NarrowboatQuest 📷

Narrowboat Chef ℗

www.narrowboatchef.com W

Neighbouring canal boats in the snow at Aston Marina.

Weights & Measures Guide

We've written our recipe book using metric measurements, so we're including this simple conversion table to help with weights and measurements, regardless of where you are in the world.

Grams – pounds & ounces

Grams	Ounces	Grams	Ounces
5g	¼ oz	225g	9 oz
10g	½ oz	250g	10 oz
25g	1 oz	275g	11 oz
50g	2 oz	300g	12 oz
75g	3 oz	325g	13 oz
100g	4 oz	350g	14 oz
125g	5 oz	375g	15 oz
150g	6 oz	400g	1 pound (lb)
175g	7 oz	700g	1½ lb
200g	8 oz	900g	2 lb

Spoons – millilitres – grams – ounces

Teaspoons	Millilitres	Grams	Ounces
1 teaspoon	5ml	5g	¼ oz
1 tablespoon	15ml	15g	¾ oz

Fresh herbs: grams - cups

We've measured fresh herbs in grams, but if you're measuring with cups, this chart may help. Using slightly more or less fresh herbs won't hugely impact a recipe.

Herb	Measurement
small leaf herbs (eg: parsley)	1 cup = approx. 50g
large leaf herbs (eg: basil)	1 cup = approx. 30g

Cups – millilitres – fluid ounces – tablespoons

Cups	Millilitres	Fluid Ounces	Tablespoons
⅛ cup	30ml	1 fl oz	2 tbsp
¼ cup	60ml	2 fl oz	4 tbsp
⅓ cup	80ml	2½ fl oz	5½ tbsp
½ cup	125ml	4 fl oz	8 tbsp
⅔ cup	160ml	5 fl oz	10½ tbsp
¾ cup	190ml	6 fl oz	12 tbsp
1 cup	250ml	8 fl oz	16 tbsp

Dry cup/tablespoon measurements – grams

Here are a few basic ingredients with dry cup and tablespoon measurements in case you prefer to measure with cups rather than grams. It's not as precise but generally won't affect the recipe much. These measurements are made using a metric cup (250ml) and metric tablespoon (15ml).

Cups/Tablespoons	Grams
1 cup of flour	170g
½ cup of flour	85g
1 cup of caster/granulated sugar	220g
½ cup of caster/granulated sugar	110g
1 cup of soft brown sugar	170g
1 cup of oats	110g
1 cup of fine couscous	180g
½ cup of fine couscous	90g
1 tablespoon of butter	10g
1 tablespoon of sugar	15g

Cooking Notes

This page contains some basic information that might come in handy as you use this cookbook.

Dietary information – we've included icons to show which recipes are friendly to certain diets. You may also see suggestions for recipes that can be easily changed to accommodate a specific dietary requirement.

 Vegetarian

Recipes with this icon are suitable for vegetarians.

 Vegan

Recipes with this icon are vegan-friendly.

 Gluten-free

Recipes with this icon do not contain gluten.

 **Cooking oil** – we haven't included specific amounts of oil, used for sweating off onions for example, in our ingredients lists. Depending on the size of your pots or pans, the amounts could vary slightly. You will find a guideline in the recipe itself as to how much oil should be on the bottom of the pan instead, otherwise between 1½ to 2 tablespoons is a good starting point for most recipes.

"Season to taste" – you've probably heard this expression before. Essentially, it means exactly what it says; taste the dish and add salt or pepper in increments until it tastes good to you. Some people prefer their meals with more pepper, others don't!

 Pepper – on the subject of seasoning, all mentions of pepper as an ingredient in this cookbook refer to finely ground black pepper unless otherwise stated.

Dry mixed Italian herbs – a staple in our kitchen is a jar of dry mixed herbs and we use them in quite a few dishes to give them a burst of flavour. If you can't get pre-mixed Italian herbs, you can make your own by combining equal parts of these dried herbs: thyme, marjoram, parsley, oregano, sage & basil.

Minced garlic – we refer to minced garlic in our recipes because we're able to buy it in a tube here (and why make more work for ourselves?). Finely chopped fresh garlic is perfectly fine to use instead if you can't get the minced stuff and you're not lazy!

Caster sugar – caster sugar isn't always readily available. It's preferred for baked goods if you can get it, but the dish certainly won't be ruined if you only have granulated sugar. Use what's available to you!

Cooking Glossary

We understand that not everyone is a chef! This page contains some basic cooking terms that we use in this cookbook and what they mean.

Al dente – an Italian term that literally translates to "to the tooth". In cooking terms, it refers to cooking your pasta to the point where it is still slightly firm in the centre when you bite into it. Taking pasta out of boiling water at this point means that by the time the pasta is served, it will be perfectly cooked.

Beating – in baking, this refers to the rigorous mixing of ingredients together to blend them and incorporate air, making baked goods light and fluffy. It can be done with a wooden spoon, electric whisk or food processor on a high speed.

Blind baking – in baking, this refers to lining raw pastry with baking paper and filling the paper with baking beads or uncooked rice and baking it. Afterwards, the beads or rice are removed and the pastry is filled. This process prevents the pastry from puffing up while pre-baking and is used when the filling needs to be cooked for less time than the pastry or when the filling doesn't need to be baked at all.

Creaming – in baking, this refers to butter and sugar being blended together thoroughly until it becomes lighter in colour and increases in volume. In our case, it's usually done with a wooden spoon, but you can use a beating attachment for a stand mixer on a medium speed.

Crimping – in baking, this refers to pressing the edges of pastry together by pinching them, usually in a fluted pattern. This seals the edges, helping to keep the contents of the pie or pastry inside while being baked.

Deglazing – adding liquid to a hot pot or pan that has browned food residue stuck to the bottom of it helps release and dissolve that flavour and bring it back into the dish. Just about any liquid will work, such as stock, wine or plain water, but the liquid used should obviously work with the rest of the recipe's flavour profile.

Folding in – in baking, this refers to gently working ingredients into each other without stirring, beating or agitating the mixture. The goal is to combine them into one mixture while still retaining as much air as possible. Use a wooden spoon or spatula to pull ingredients from the bottom of the bowl up and over the ingredients on top repeatedly, until the ingredients are combined.

Sweating – this refers to gently cooking ingredients in a pot or pan with a small amount of oil or butter over a low to medium heat.

Terminology Differences

Sometimes there are differences in the names of ingredients or tools used in cooking depending on where you live. This list might help if you find yourself wondering what's what.

Plain flour	All-purpose flour
Self-raising flour	Self-rising flour
Strong flour	Bread flour
Wholemeal flour	Whole wheat flour
Bicarbonate of soda	Baking soda
Black treacle	Molasses
Caster sugar	Superfine sugar
Icing sugar	Confectioner's sugar/powdered sugar
Double cream	Heavy cream
Sultanas	Seedless golden raisins
Biscuits	Cookies
Scones	Biscuits
Digestive biscuits	Graham crackers
Butternut squash	Butternut pumpkin
Red/green/yellow pepper	Capsicum/bell pepper
Mange tout	Snow peas
Spring onions	Scallions
Swede	Rutabaga
Coriander	Cilantro
Corn flour	Cornstarch
Beef mince	Ground beef
Tomato paste	Tomato purée
Tomato passata	Strained tomato purée
Baking paper	Parchment paper
Pan/frying pan	Skillet
Grill/grilling	Broil/broiling
Kitchen towel	Paper towel/kitchen roll

Essential Recipes

Some of the recipes in this cookbook call for ingredients such as 'stock.' We tend to use gel stock pots, or you can use powdered stock or bouillon. Alternatively, if you have the space and resources, you can make your own stocks.

Basic beef stock

makes approx. 2 litres

- 1 kg beef bones
- 60g onions, unpeeled and roughly chopped
- 100g carrots, unpeeled and roughly chopped
- 40g celery, roughly chopped
- 2.5 litres cold water
- 2 bay leaves (optional)
- 6 peppercorns (optional)

1. Brown the bones and vegetables in an oven on medium heat for about 20-30 minutes.
2. Place the bones and vegetables in a stock pot, drain any excess fat from the roasting tray and use some hot water to get any browned meat juices from the tray and pour into the stock pot.
3. Add the water, bring to the boil and skim off any scum that rises to the surface.
4. Add bay leaves and peppercorns and drop the temperature to a simmer. Simmer for 4-5 hours.
5. Skim any scum from the surface, then strain and throw away the solids. Use stock within 3 days, or freeze for future use.

Basic chicken stock

Use the same amount of ingredients as the beef stock, but replace beef bones with chicken bones. Skip step 1 and start at **step 2**, then follow the rest of the steps, but only simmer it for 3-4 hours.

Basic vegetable stock

- 2 onions, unpeeled and roughly chopped
- 3 carrots, unpeeled and roughly chopped
- 4 celery stalks, roughly chopped
- 1 bay leaf
- 4 peppercorns

1. Place all ingredients into a stock pot and fill with cold water until vegetables are covered with about 5cm (2 inches) of water.
2. Bring to a simmer and simmer for about 1 hour, stirring occasionally.
3. Strain the stock and throw away the solids. Use within 3 days or freeze for future use.

Mayonnaise

makes approx. 250ml

- 2 egg yolks
- 1 teaspoon vinegar
- 1 teaspoon Dijon mustard
- 250ml oil
- salt and pepper to taste

1. Place the egg yolks, vinegar and mustard in a mixing bowl and whisk well.
2. Gradually add the oil very slowly while continuously whisking. Continue until all the oil is incorporated.
3. Season to taste.

- Any vegetable oil can be used, but olive oil produces the best results.
- If the mayonnaise becomes too thick, whisk a small amount of vinegar or water through it.
- Adding the oil too quickly will cause the sauce to split. You can redeem split mayonnaise by whisking another egg yolk in a clean bowl, then slowly whisking in the split sauce.

Easy aioli

Also known as garlic mayonnaise, aioli is essentially mayonnaise with garlic added to it. Make a batch of mayonnaise as above, then whisk in 1 tablespoon of lemon juice and 1 tablespoon of minced garlic. For best results, the garlic must be a paste in order to properly permeate the mayonnaise.

Tartare sauce

Normally served with fish dishes, tartare sauce is a mayonnaise derivative. After making a batch of mayonnaise, mix in 25g roughly chopped capers, 35g roughly chopped gherkins and 15g of finely chopped parsley.

Thickening agent

Sometimes to make a sauce or stew nice and thick without having to reduce it, we use a thickening agent. Our preferred method is 1 tablespoon of corn flour (cornstarch) whisked into 100ml of cold water. Corn flour has a neutral flavour profile so it's perfect.

This method also works using 1 tablespoon of gravy powder to 100ml of cold water – this will help give beef-based sauces a richer flavour.

Take note that you may not need the whole amount of thickening agent. Add it bit by bit and wait for a minute between adding to allow it to work. When the sauce has reached your desired consistency, you can stop adding the thickening agent.

My Notes

_____

_____

_____

_____

_____

_____

_____

_____

_____

_____

_____

_____

Soups, Sides & Small Meals

Butternut Squash & Sage Soup

One of our favourite autumnal soups is this lush butternut squash soup with its delightful hint of sage. The lovely orange colour is the perfect accompaniment to the season of rich golden colours!

SERVES 4

DIETARY INFO:

- 1 large butternut squash
- 1 large brown onion
- 3 celery stalks
- 25g butter
- 20g fresh sage
- 1 tablespoon dry mixed Italian herbs
- 800ml chicken or vegetable stock
- salt and pepper to taste
- soured cream to serve

 Make this recipe vegan-friendly by substituting the butter with a plant-based margarine and either leaving off the soured cream at the end or replacing it with soy cream.

1. Preheat the oven to 200°c (400°f/gas mark 6). Peel, deseed and cut the squash into medium chunks of similar sizes. Cut the onion and celery into medium dice.

2. Spread the squash on an oven tray, sprinkle with oil and season generously with salt and pepper. Roast for 25 minutes or until tender.

3. When the squash is almost ready, start the soup base. In a large pot over medium heat, add enough oil to cover the base of the pot, add the butter with the onion and celery and cook for a few minutes until softened. Add the dried herbs and the sage and cook for a further 1-2 minutes.

4. Remove the squash from the oven when ready, add it straight to the pot and turn the heat up to high. Add the stock, bring it to the boil, then reduce the heat and allow it to simmer for 10 minutes.

5. Using a stick blender or food processor, blend the soup until it is smooth and season to taste.

6. Serve hot, garnished with some soured cream and fresh sage leaves.

Saag Aloo

This Indian side dish is the perfect blend of spinach, potato and fragrant spices. It's always well-received on our narrowboat! We enjoy having it as a side to other curries or simply eating it with flat breads.

🍴 **SERVES 2**   **DIETARY INFO:**

- 500g potatoes
- 1 brown onion
- 1 teaspoon minced ginger
- 1 teaspoon minced garlic
- 50g butter
- 1 teaspoon ground cumin
- 1 teaspoon ground turmeric
- 1 teaspoon garam masala
- 1 medium red chilli
- 300g baby spinach
- salt and pepper to taste

 Make this recipe vegan-friendly by substituting the butter with a plant-based margarine.

1. Cut the potatoes into large chunks and boil them for 12-15 minutes until they're just beginning to soften. When they're ready, drain them and set them aside to steam off residual moisture.

2. Meanwhile, finely dice the onion and red chilli. In a hot pot over medium heat, add enough oil to cover the base of the pot and begin sweating the onions. Add the ginger and garlic and cook for 1-2 minutes while stirring.

3. Turn the heat up to high, add the butter and let it melt then mix in the spices and continue cooking for another 1-2 minutes.

4. Add the potatoes to the pot and stir, ensuring they get well coated with the onion and spice mix. Add in the chilli and stir through, then remove from the heat and mix in the spinach, using the residual heat to wilt it.

5. Season to taste with salt and pepper. Serve while hot either on its own with naan bread or as a side dish.

Creamy Mashed Potato

Who doesn't love a decadently smooth and creamy mash? Considering the simple ingredients, this side dish is ridiculously easy to make and the perfect accompaniment to many winter dishes.

 SERVES 4

DIETARY INFO:

- 600g potatoes
- 60ml cream
- 50g butter
- salt and pepper to taste

 Make this recipe vegan-friendly by substituting the butter with a plant-based margarine and the cream with soy cream.

1. Peel and cut the potatoes into medium chunks of similar sizes. Place them in a pot and fill it with water until the potatoes are covered by at least 2½ cm (1 inch). Add a generous pinch of salt to the water.

2. Bring the water to the boil, then reduce to a simmer. Cover with a lid and cook for 15-20 minutes, or until you can easily poke a fork through the potatoes.

3. While the potatoes are cooking, melt the butter and warm the cream together in a small pot, then remove from the heat.

4. When the potatoes are done, drain the water and leave the hot potatoes in their pot. Pour the butter and cream mix over them.

5. Mash the potatoes with a potato masher, then finish them off by beating them with a kitchen spoon or spatula. Don't over-beat them or they will become gluey.

6. Season to taste with salt and pepper and serve.

Mini Quiches

These little pastries are perfect finger food for parties and events or just as a tasty snack to nibble on, hot or cold. They're versatile and can be filled with a huge variety of ingredients. Use your creativity!

 Makes 9 mini quiches

Dietary Info:

Shortcrust pastry

- 200g plain flour
- 100g softened butter
- 2-3 tablespoons water
- ½ teaspoon salt

Quiche mix

- 3 eggs
- 150ml milk
- 150ml cream
- salt and pepper to taste

Quiche filling suggestions

- bacon and cheese
- feta and olive
- semi dried tomato, basil and cheese
- caramelised red onion and goats cheese
- red pepper and onion
- spinach and ricotta

You can use store-bought shortcrust pastry if you like, or follow these steps to make your own.

1. Put the flour and butter into a mixing bowl and rub together until combined. Dissolve the salt into the water and gradually add it to the flour while mixing until the dough sticks together.

2. Form dough into a flat disc, cover with plastic wrap and leave in the fridge for half an hour to set.

3. Meanwhile, prepare your desired quiche fillings and preheat the oven to 190°c (375°f/gas mark 5).

4. Remove the dough from the fridge and roll out on a floured surface. The dough should be rolled to roughly 4-5mm thickness (just under ¼ of an inch).

5. Find a cutter, lid or cup that will create the right size circles to fill your muffin tin. Cut circles from the dough and gently press them into the muffin tin (no greasing needed). Score the base of the pastry lightly with a knife.

6. Blind bake the pastry for 12-13 minutes.

7. While the pastry is baking, add the eggs, milk and cream to a mixing bowl and whisk together. Season with salt and pepper and set aside.

8. Check the pastry – it should be starting to firm up and turn golden at the edges. Remove the blind baking implements and put the pastry back into the oven for 2-3 minutes to finish the base.

9. Once the pastry is baked, remove it from the oven and fill each case halfway with the egg mix. Add in your chosen quiche fillings and seasonings and top up with the remaining egg mix until it reaches just below the rim of the pastry cases.

10. Put them back in the oven for 10-15 minutes until the egg is cooked through.

11. Serve hot or cold as party food, as a meal with a fresh salad, or even just as a snack!

Autumn colours on the
Trent & Mersey canal.

Bringing Andrea Rose into the top lock at Stoke-on-Trent.

Misty morning in Aston Marina.

Potato & Bacon Soup

Potatoes are such a cost effective, filling staple in many peoples' pantries. This recipe makes a large batch, perfect for freezing or having in the fridge for a quickly-heated meal after a long, muddy walk along the towpath.

SERVES 6

DIETARY INFO:

- 1kg washed potatoes
- 2 brown onions
- 3 leeks
- 3 sticks of celery
- 30g butter
- 2 teaspoons minced garlic
- 1 tablespoon dry mixed Italian herbs
- 1.25 litres chicken stock
- 300g smoked bacon
- salt and pepper to taste

 Make this recipe vegetarian and vegan-friendly by turning it into a simple potato and leek soup – remove the bacon, substitute the butter with a plant-based margarine and the chicken stock with vegetable stock.

1. Roughly chop the vegetables into similar sized chunks.

2. In a large pot over medium heat, add enough oil to easily cover the base of the pot. Sweat the onions, celery and leeks. Turn the heat to high, add the butter and garlic and cook for 1-2 minutes.

3. Add the potatoes and the mixed herbs. Stir and add the stock. Bring it to the boil, reduce the heat to a simmer and put the lid on. Simmer for about 15 minutes.

4. While the soup is cooking, dice the bacon into roughly 1cm (½ inch) pieces and fry off in a hot pan with a small amount of oil until it starts to brown. Remove from the heat and set aside.

5. Once the potatoes are soft, blitz the soup with a hand blender or food processor until smooth. Add the bacon to the soup and stir through.

6. Season with salt and pepper to taste. Best served hot with warm homemade bread – try our bread recipe on **page 48**.

Mushroom Melts

When wild mushrooms start springing up along the towpath, we know autumn is upon us. We're not brave enough or knowledgable enough to use any of the mushrooms we see though... We buy them from the store!

 SERVES 2

DIETARY INFO:

- 4 field mushrooms
- 1 tablespoon vegetable oil
- 1 red onion, finely sliced
- 50g butter
- 1 teaspoon sugar
- 75ml balsamic vinegar
- 50g mozzarella, grated
- 50g cheddar, grated
- salt and pepper to taste
- balsamic glaze to garnish

1. Preheat the oven to 180°c (350°f/gas mark 4).

2. Spread mushrooms out on a baking tray and drizzle the vegetable oil over them. Sprinkle with a small amount of salt and pepper and cook in the oven for about 15 minutes.

3. In a pan over medium heat, add just enough oil to cover the base of the pan. When hot, add the onions and begin sweating them. When they start to soften, add the butter, season with salt and pepper to taste, then sprinkle the sugar over.

4. Cook the onions while stirring often for 20-25 minutes until they have gone a deep golden brown.

5. Deglaze the pan with the balsamic vinegar and continue to cook for another 1-2 minutes before removing from the heat.

6. Top the mushrooms with the caramelised onions and top with the grated cheese.

7. Place under a grill for 2-3 minutes to melt the cheese. Serve hot with a drizzle of balsamic glaze on top.

Arancini Balls

These little balls of flavour have a fancy name – but they're essentially just risotto rolled into a ball, crumbed and deep fried! Or in other words, a fantastically delicious way to use up leftover risotto!

 SERVES 4

DIETARY INFO:

- approx. 400g cooked risotto (see **page 76**)
- 150g plain flour
- 150g breadcrumbs
- 3 eggs
- 50ml milk
- vegetable oil for frying

1. If you don't have leftover risotto for these, follow steps 4-7 from our butternut squash risotto recipe on **page 76**. Place the risotto in the fridge to cool for at least 3 hours, preferably overnight.

2. Divide and roll the cooled risotto into equal portions about the size of a golf ball.

3. Put the flour and breadcrumbs into separate bowls. In a third bowl, whisk the eggs and milk together.

4. Dip each risotto ball into the flour, followed by the egg mix, and finally the breadcrumbs, ensuring they are well coated. Place them onto a tray and put them in the fridge to set for about 15 minutes.

5. Pour about 4cm (1½ inches) of vegetable oil into a deep pot and bring it up to a high heat. Place the risotto balls carefully into the oil in batches and cook for 8-10 minutes until golden on all sides. Drain on kitchen towel to remove excess oil.

6. Eat the arancini balls warm or cold on their own as a finger food, or serve with almost any type of pasta sauce.

French Onion Soup

This recipe was chosen by one of our Patreons, Judy – she sent us her amazing French onion soup recipe. We've tweaked it to add our own touches and make it easier for us to cook aboard our narrowboat!

 SERVES 4

- 1kg brown onions
- 50g butter
- 2 tablespoons plain flour
- 2 teaspoons dry mixed Italian herbs
- 150ml dry white wine
- 1.3 litres beef stock
- 4-8 slices baguette bread
- 150g cheese, finely grated

Judy says:

"There are two secrets to making a delicious French onion soup: make your own beef stock and cook your onions on low heat for a really long time."

*See **page 14** for our beef stock recipe.*

1. Thinly slice the onions. (Yes, you will probably be crying by the end of it!)

2. In a large pot over low heat, add enough oil to cover the base of the pot and add the onions and butter. Begin gently frying them – if they burn they will go bitter and spoil the soup, so try to avoid that!

3. Keep the heat low and continue cooking the onions for 2 hours, stirring occasionally. They will start to darken as they caramelise.

4. Stir in the plain flour and dry herbs. Increase the heat to high and gradually add the wine, stirring continuously. Add the beef stock and stir, then reduce the heat to a simmer. Simmer for about 15 minutes.

5. While the soup is simmering, toast the baguette slices under a grill.

6. Ladle the soup into heat resistant bowls, place a slice or two of the toasted baguette on top of the soup, top with the cheese and place the whole concoction back under the grill until the cheese is melted and golden. Serve immediately.

Frosted morning in
Aston Marina.

Golden leaves over a lock near
the town of Stone.

Beautiful English house overlooking the Trent & Mersey Canal.

Crispy Fried Chicken Strips

The perfect recipe for when you're craving some deep-fried goodness!
Don't be overwhelmed by the number of ingredients in this one – it's mainly comprised of spices and you can choose your favourites if you prefer.

 SERVES 4

- 400g chicken breasts
- 3 eggs
- 50ml milk
- 100g plain flour
- vegetable oil for frying

Spiced crumb mix

- 100g breadcrumbs
- 70g plain flour
- 1 teaspoon onion powder
- 1 teaspoon garlic powder
- 2 teaspoons unsmoked paprika
- 1 teaspoon dried oregano
- 1 teaspoon ground cumin
- ½ teaspoon cayenne pepper
- ½ teaspoon salt
- ½ teaspoon pepper

Honey mustard sauce

- 1½ tablespoons honey
- 1 tablespoon Dijon mustard
- 1 tablespoon seeded mustard
- 5 tablespoons mayonnaise

1. Whisk the ingredients for the honey mustard sauce together in a bowl and set aside.

2. Slice the chicken breasts into strips about 2cm (¾ inch) wide.

3. Put the 100g of flour in a shallow bowl. In another bowl, mix all the ingredients for the spiced crumb mix together. In a third bowl, whisk the eggs and the milk together.

4. Dip each chicken strip into the flour, followed by the egg mixture, and finally the spiced crumb mix, making sure they are all well coated.

5. Pour about 4cm (1½ inches) of vegetable oil into a deep pot and bring it up to a high heat. Carefully place the breaded chicken into the oil and cook in several batches for 7-9 minutes, or until they are a deep golden brown. Place onto kitchen towel to absorb excess oil.

6. Serve hot with the honey mustard dipping sauce on the side.

Cream of Mushroom Soup

A tasty soup that is quick and easy to prepare after a cold morning working locks along the canal. We used tame mushrooms bought from the store, but if you know your mushrooms, feel free to harvest your own for a cream of *wild* mushroom soup!

SERVES 4

- 700g white mushrooms
- 1 brown onion
- 100g butter
- 2 teaspoons minced garlic
- 1 teaspoon dried thyme
- 2 tablespoons plain flour
- 600ml chicken stock
- 100ml cream
- salt and pepper to taste

Make this recipe vegetarian and vegan-friendly by substituting the chicken stock with vegetable stock, the butter with a plant-based margarine and the cream with soy cream.

*Make this recipe gluten-free by using the corn flour thickening agent recipe on **page 15**. Add this gradually to the blitzed soup until at your desired thickness.*

1. Roughly dice the onions and slice the mushrooms.

2. In a large pot over medium heat, add enough oil to cover the base and begin sweating the onions. When the onions have started to soften, add the butter, mushrooms and garlic, stir and cook for about 4 minutes.

3. Add the thyme and sprinkle the flour over the mushrooms. Stir through.

4. Add the stock, bring to a simmer and continue simmering for 6-7 minutes. Stir the cream through.

5. Remove from the heat and blitz the soup with a stick blender or food processor until smooth. Season to taste and serve.

Homemade Chips

We're absolutely in love with these simple, homemade hot chips – especially when they're dipped in aioli sauce. This recipe uses plain white potatoes, but we've also used sweet potatoes and they are divine! Why not try both?

 SERVES 4   DIETARY INFO:

- 4 large washed potatoes
- 1 tablespoon onion powder
- 2 tablespoons vegetable oil
- ½ teaspoon salt
- ½ teaspoon pepper

If you want to make the sweet potato variety, cut the potatoes a little larger than you would for the white potatoes – sweet potato chips shrink a lot more than the normal ones do.

1. Preheat the oven to 200°c (400°f/gas mark 6).

2. Cut the potatoes into long batons about 1½ cm (½ inch) wide and deep. They need to look like chips, basically!

3. Place the cut potato into a bowl and add the vegetable oil, onion powder, salt and pepper. Toss together, ensuring the chips are evenly coated.

4. Spread the chips onto a baking tray and cook in the oven for about 45 minutes, turning them every 10-15 minutes to ensure all sides are cooked evenly.

5. Serve the chips hot out of the oven. We love eating them with a side of aioli dipping sauce. We have a simple recipe for aioli on **page 15**.

Spinach & Camembert Pastry Puffs

Spinach and ricotta are often paired together – why not try something different with these spinach and camembert puffs? The creamy camembert cheese combined with the flaky puff pastry makes these such a tasty treat.

 SERVES 2

DIETARY INFO:

- 1 roll of puff pastry (approx. 320g)
- 400g baby spinach
- 75g butter
- 200g camembert cheese
- salt and pepper to taste
- milk for brushing

Make this recipe gluten-free by using gluten-free puff pastry.

1. Preheat the oven to 190°c (375°f/gas mark 5).

2. In a medium pot over high heat, add just enough oil to cover the base of the pot and melt the butter. Add the spinach and stir around the pot for a minute, coating it in the butter. Season with salt and pepper.

3. Turn the heat off and cover the pot with a lid for 1-2 minutes to finish wilting the spinach. Slice the camembert into 5mm (¼ inch) wide slices and set aside.

4. Cut the puff pastry into even squares – the size of them doesn't really matter. Place a slice of camembert cheese on one side of an imaginary line running diagonally through the centre of the pastry square. Leave about 1cm (½ inch) from the cheese to the edges of the pastry.

5. Cover the cheese with wilted spinach, then brush the edges of the pastry with milk. Fold one of the corners to the opposite corner to form a triangle and press down firmly where the edges meet to seal the triangle.

6. Carefully lift the triangles onto a lined tray and use a fork to crimp the edges. Brush the tops of the parcels with milk and use a knife to make two small slits in the top.

7. Place in the oven for 15-20 minutes until they become golden and puffy. Leave for a minute after removing from the oven, then serve.

White Cob Loaf

This bread loaf is very simple and easy to make. If you're feeling particularly brave, you could shape the dough into buns, or even into two small loaves, hollow them out and serve one of our soup recipes inside!

 SERVES 4

DIETARY INFO:

- 300g strong white bread flour
- 1 teaspoon dry yeast
- ½ teaspoon sugar
- ½ teaspoon salt
- 200ml warm water
- ½ tablespoon sesame seeds for top

1. Put the flour into a mixing bowl and add the yeast and sugar on one side and the salt on the opposite side.

2. Add the warm water and mix until all the flour is combined. Add extra water if needed. The dough should be slightly sticky, but still come away from the edges of the bowl easily.

3. Cover the dough with plastic to form an airtight seal and leave to rise for a few hours until it has almost doubled in size.

4. After the bread has risen, sprinkle flour on a flat surface and knead the dough, just for about 1 minute. Place it back into the bowl, cover and let it rise again for about 1 hour.

5. When it's ready to bake, preheat the oven to 200°c (400°f/gas mark 6). Form the dough into a round ball shape and place on a baking tray. Brush some water over the top and sprinkle it with sesame seeds. Bake in the oven for 20-25 minutes.

6. When the bread is ready, it should be golden brown and crispy on top. Remove from the oven and leave to cool. Enjoy it either warm or cold.

Garlic Herb Bread

Back in Australia, our Christmas table wouldn't be complete if it didn't include fresh garlic bread! It's a great side dish to serve with pastas – or anything really because let's be honest, garlic bread is awesome!

SERVES 4

DIETARY INFO:

- 300g strong white bread flour
- 1 teaspoon dry yeast
- ½ teaspoon sugar
- ½ teaspoon salt
- 1 tablespoon dry mixed Italian herbs
- 1 teaspoon onion powder
- 200ml warm water

Garlic butter

- 50g softened butter
- 1 teaspoon minced garlic

 Make this recipe vegan-friendly by substituting the butter with a plant-based margarine.

1. Put the flour into a mixing bowl and add the yeast and sugar on one side and the salt on the opposite side. Add the dry herbs and the onion powder.

2. Add the warm water and mix until all the flour is combined. Add extra water if needed. The dough should be slightly sticky, but still come away from the edges of the bowl easily.

3. Cover the dough with plastic to form an airtight seal and leave to rise for a few hours until it has almost doubled in size.

4. Preheat the oven to 200°c (400°f/gas mark 6). Tip the dough out onto a floured surface and gently form it into a slightly rounded rectangular shape that's about 4cm (1½ inches) high. Put it on a tray, let it sit for half an hour, then bake for 15-18 minutes.

5. While the bread is baking, make the garlic butter by mixing the garlic into the softened butter until well combined.

6. Remove the bread from the oven and let it sit for 10 minutes to cool slightly. Cut the loaf at about 2cm (1 inch) intervals along the length of the bread, making sure to not cut all the way through, leaving the slices connected at the bottom.

7. Spread both sides of the slices generously with garlic butter, put the loaf back in the oven for about 7-10 minutes, then serve hot.

Seeded Loaf

When everything has gone to seed, turn it into bread!
This is an easy recipe; we're sure that you will 'suc-*seed*' with it.
(Puns courtesy of Maggie's Aunt Sue...)

 SERVES 6   DIETARY INFO:

- 300g strong white bread flour
- 200g wholemeal flour
- 2 teaspoons dry yeast
- 1 teaspoon sugar
- 1 teaspoon salt
- 300ml warm water
- 2 tablespoons oil
- 100g mixed seeds

1. Put the flours into a mixing bowl and add the yeast and sugar on one side and the salt on the opposite side.

2. Add the warm water and oil and mix until all the flour is combined. Add extra water if needed. The dough should be slightly sticky, but still come away from the edges of the bowl easily.

3. Mix the seeds through the dough, then cover the bowl with plastic wrap so that it's airtight and leave for an hour to rise or until it has almost doubled in size.

4. Turn the dough out onto a floured surface and knead for about 5 minutes. Shape into a rough rectangular shape and place into a greased loaf tin. Cover and leave to rise for another hour.

5. When ready to bake, preheat the oven to 200°c (400°f/gas mark 6).

6. Bake for 30-35 minutes. The top should be golden brown and crispy when it's ready. You can also test if it's cooked through the same way you would test a cake – poke a skewer into the centre and if it comes out clean, it's ready. If sticky dough is on the skewer the bread needs to cook longer.

7. Remove from the oven and leave to cool in the tin for about 10 minutes, then remove from the tin and let it finish cooling – or enjoy fresh warm bread!

Pixel enjoying a walk along
the towpath!

Main Meals

Carbonara

This is one of the best carbonara recipes we've ever made. We used to make our carbonara based on cream but then we tried an egg version and haven't looked back! We think this carbonara beats all others!

 SERVES 2

- 2 whole eggs
- 2 egg yolks
- 60g parmesan cheese
- 250g spaghetti
- 170g smoked pancetta, roughly diced
- salt and pepper to taste
- half a spring onion to garnish, finely chopped

1. Put a pot of water with a generous pinch of salt on to boil for the spaghetti.

2. While waiting, finely grate or powder the parmesan cheese. Put the eggs and egg yolks into a large mixing bowl, add the parmesan and about ½ teaspoon of pepper and lightly whisk together.

3. When the water is boiling, add the spaghetti and cook until it is *al dente*.

4. While the pasta is cooking, fry off the pancetta in a hot pan with a very small amount of oil over high heat for about 8-10 minutes until it starts to brown.

5. When the pasta is ready, drain the the water and add the pasta to the pan with the pancetta. Toss the pancetta through the pasta and turn off the heat.

6. Transfer the pasta and pancetta into the mixing bowl with the eggs and mix all the ingredients together with tongs, using the residual heat of the pasta and pancetta to cook the eggs out.

7. Season to taste with salt and pepper and serve. Garnish with some grated parmesan and chopped spring onion.

Pan Fried Salmon with Crushed Potatoes

We don't eat fish often, but when we do we enjoy succulent
salmon fillets served with potatoes and asparagus – plus a decadent
lemon butter sauce to top it all off!

 SERVES 2

DIETARY INFO:

- 2 salmon fillets (approx. 130g-150g each)
- 300g washed potatoes
- 30g butter
- 30ml cream
- 10 asparagus spears
- 75ml lemon juice
- salt and pepper to taste

1. Cut the potatoes into large chunks, leaving the skin on. Put them into a pot and fill it with water until they are covered by at least 2½ cm (1 inch). Bring it to the boil and cook them for 10-15 minutes until they start to turn soft.

2. Drain the water and let the potatoes sit and dry out for a few minutes. In the same pot they were cooked in, add the cream and 10g of the butter to the potatoes. Using a potato masher, crush the potatoes briefly, leaving small chunks. Season to taste.

3. Bring a pot of water to the boil and add a generous pinch of salt. Add the asparagus and cook for 4-5 minutes.

4. Over high heat, add just enough oil to lightly coat a frying pan. Season the flesh side of the salmon fillets with salt and pepper. When the pan is hot, place them into the pan, seasoned side down. Cook for about 3 minutes until lightly brown. Gently turn them over and cook for a further 3 minutes.

5. Remove the salmon from the pan and plate it up with the potatoes and asparagus.

6. In the same pan over low heat, add the remaining butter and melt it. When it starts to bubble add the lemon juice and move the sauce around the pan and cook for 30-40 seconds. Pour the sauce over the salmon and serve.

Lamb Stew

Lamb is expensive, however we get around this by using the cheaper diced lamb to create this delicious stew. Simply add in some vegetables and you're ready to go! Perfect after a cold autumn day of narrowboat cruising!

 SERVES 4

- 500g diced lamb
- 85g plain flour
- 1 large onion, medium dice
- 3 sticks of celery, medium dice
- 10g butter
- 1 tablespoon minced garlic
- 3 medium carrots, cut into half circles
- 125ml red wine
- 4 medium potatoes, cut into bite-size chunks
- 800ml lamb or beef stock
- 80g fine green beans, trimmed and halved
- 1 teaspoon dry mixed Italian herbs
- 1 teaspoon dried rosemary
- 1 teaspoon dried thyme
- 2 tablespoons gravy powder
- 100ml cold water
- salt and pepper to taste

1. Place the flour into a shallow bowl and mix a pinch of salt and pepper into it. Roll the diced lamb in the flour to give it a light coating.

2. Add oil to a large pot over high heat until it generously covers the base of the pot. Seal the diced lamb until golden brown on all sides and remove from the pot. Seal the meat in several batches so the pot doesn't become overloaded. Set the browned meat aside.

3. Lower the heat to medium, and into the same pot add more oil if it's dry and add the onions and celery and start sweating them. After a minute, add the butter and minced garlic and continue cooking until the onions start to soften.

4. Turn the heat to high, add the carrots to the pot and stir, cooking for about two minutes, then add the red wine to deglaze the pan. Let it work its magic for a minute or two.

5. Stir in the sealed lamb and the potatoes. Add the lamb/beef stock. Bring the stew to the boil while gently stirring, then turn the heat down to a simmer. Place a lid on the pot and leave to stew for about 30-40 minutes.

6. After the 30-40 minutes of stewing, stir in the green beans and the dried herbs.

7. Whisk the gravy powder into the cold water. Add it gradually to the stew while stirring until you have the desired thickness. Season with salt and pepper to taste (gravy powder is usually quite salty so you may not need salt).

8. Serve hot with some crusty homemade cob loaf from **page 48** in our starters section!

Pixel bounding along a frozen jetty in Aston Marina!

Cruising through a flight of locks near Stoke-on-Trent.

Gorgeous trees growing
at the edge of the canal.

Crispy Teriyaki Chicken Rice Bowls

The inspiration for these rice bowls came from the sushi train restaurants back in Australia. Ryan always used to order one of these bowls! They're a little more work than our average recipe, but definitely worth it!

 SERVES 2

DIETARY INFO:

- 400g chicken thigh
- 175ml soy sauce
- 1 teaspoon minced ginger
- 1 teaspoon minced garlic
- ½ teaspoon pepper
- 1 tablespoon sesame oil
- 75ml sake
- 75ml rice wine vinegar/ mirin
- 40g caster sugar
- 100g corn flour + 2 tablespoons for thickening
- 2 cups uncooked Japanese medium grain rice
- 4 cups water + 100ml cold water for thickening
- mayonnaise

1. Cut the chicken into bite-sized pieces.

2. In a bowl mix 100ml of the soy sauce, the ginger, garlic, pepper and sesame oil together, then add the chicken thigh. Cover and place into the fridge for 20-30 minutes to marinate.

3. To make the teriyaki sauce combine the remaining soy sauce, the sake, rice wine vinegar and sugar in a small pot and place it over medium heat. Stir for a few minutes until the sugar dissolves.

4. Whisk together the 2 tablespoons of corn flour and 100ml cold water and add it gradually to the teriyaki sauce to thicken it. You'll know it's thick enough when it lightly coats the back of a spoon. Remove it from the heat and set aside.

5. Rinse the rice until the water runs clear. Add the rice into a medium-sized pot and add the 4 cups of water (or enough water that when you touch the rice the water comes up to the first knuckle of your index finger).

6. Cover the pot with a lid and bring the rice to the boil. Once boiling, turn the heat down low and let the rice simmer for 15-20 minutes. Make sure to keep the lid on the whole time.

7. Pour about 4cm (1½ inches) of vegetable oil into a deep pot and bring it up to a high heat.

8. Place the 100g of corn flour into a shallow bowl and cover the marinated chicken in a light coating, then fry 4-5 pieces at a time for 3-4 minutes until they are a deep golden brown colour. Remove them from the oil and let them drain on a wire rack or kitchen towel.

9. Split the rice evenly between two bowls and top with the chicken pieces. Finish the dish off by drizzling it all with the teriyaki sauce and a drizzle of mayonnaise. Serve immediately.

Vegetable Udon Noodle Soup

We're fond of our Asian-inspired dishes. Both of us love meals based on noodles and rice – to the point that Ryan insists he can't do without his power-hungry rice cooker! Luckily, this dish doesn't require it!

 SERVES 2

DIETARY INFO:

- 1 carrot, peeled
- 100g sweet corn
- 6 tenderstem broccoli
- 6 mange tout
- mixed Asian mushrooms, roughly chopped
- 800ml vegetable stock
- 2 tablespoons soy sauce
- 1 tablespoon sesame oil + 1 teaspoon for finishing
- 300g udon noodles
- 2 boiled eggs
- 1 teaspoon sesame seeds
- pepper to taste

Make this recipe vegan-friendly by leaving out the boiled eggs.

1. Slice the carrot into thin circles and blanch them for a minute in boiling water, then cool them immediately in cold water. If using frozen corn, place it into the boiling water for 2-3 minutes, then remove. Trim excess stem from the broccoli and place into the boiling water for 2-3 minutes, then remove. Thinly slice the mange tout and set all vegetables and mushrooms aside.

2. In a medium-sized pot heat the vegetable stock to a simmer and add the soy sauce, the tablespoon of sesame oil and pepper to taste to make the soup.

3. Put the udon noodles into a separate pot of boiling water, cook them for about 2 minutes, then drain.

4. Place ½ a teaspoon of sesame oil into the bottom of each serving bowl and add a few ladles of hot soup. Divide the noodles evenly between the bowls and cover with more soup.

5. Cut the boiled eggs in half. Place the tenderstem broccoli, mushrooms, carrot, corn, mange tout and eggs into the bowls and finish with a sprinkle of sesame seeds.

Braised Pepper Steaks

We love using our coal-fueled fireplace as an alternative cooking space.
It's got just enough space on the top of it to sit a casserole dish and slow
cook these delicious braised steaks. Two birds with one stone!

 SERVES 2

- 2 braising steaks (cheaper, tougher meat)
- 50g plain flour
- 1 brown onion, finely diced
- 1 teaspoon minced garlic
- 100g green peppercorns
- 1 teaspoon dried oregano
- ½ teaspoon dried thyme
- 1 tablespoon tomato paste
- 100ml red wine
- 400ml beef stock
- 2 tablespoons corn flour/gravy powder
- 100ml cold water
- salt and pepper to taste

1. Preheat the oven to 140°c (275°f/gas mark 1).

2. Place the flour into a shallow bowl and mix in a generous pinch of both salt and pepper. Cover the steaks in a light coating of flour.

3. Use a casserole dish or baking tray that is just large enough to fit the two steaks lying flat. Heat the dish over high heat on the stove, add just enough oil to cover the base and seal the steaks off until both sides are browned. Remove from the dish and set aside.

4. Lower the heat to medium and if the dish is dry, add a little more oil and start sweating the onions. When they have started to soften, add the garlic and the green peppercorns and cook for a minute.

5. Turn the heat up to high, add the dried herbs and the tomato paste to the dish, stir and cook for another minute.

6. Deglaze the dish with the red wine, using a wooden spoon to scrape the bottom of the dish and loosen any flavour stuck to the bottom. Add the beef stock and bring to a simmer.

7. Once simmering, turn the stove off and add the steaks into the dish, ensuring they are fully covered by the liquid.

8. Place a lid on the dish or cover it with tinfoil and put it in the oven for 1½ hours or until the meat is tender.

9. Once tender, remove the dish from the oven, take the steaks out of the braising liquid and set aside.

10. Bring the liquid up to a simmer on the stove top. Whisk the corn flour/gravy powder with the cold water and use it to thicken the braising liquid. Season to taste with salt and pepper.

11. Serve the steaks with mashed potato (see **page 24**) and steamed vegetables and generous amounts of the braising sauce.

Spiced Chickpea & Root Veg Salad

Our Patreon, Craig, suggested this salad. Salads tend to be associated with more summery, warm-weather dishes, but this hearty, spiced salad is perfect for the cooler months. It's a lovely meal to enjoy on a crisp autumn afternoon on the narrowboat.

 SERVES 2

DIETARY INFO:

- 1 teaspoon ground cumin
- 1 teaspoon garam masala
- ½ teaspoon ground coriander
- 1 parsnip
- 1 small sweet potato
- 1 large carrot
- ½ a swede
- 400g (240g drained weight) tinned chickpeas
- 2 tablespoons olive oil
- ½ red onion, thinly sliced
- mixed lettuce leaves
- salt and pepper to taste

Craig says:
"I'm the cook in my family, but my busy job as a paramedic means I like meals that are hearty but easy to throw together. The leftovers make a great lunch to take to work the next day as well."

1. Preheat the oven to 200°c (400°f/gas mark 6). Mix the spices together and set aside.

2. Cut the parsnip, sweet potato, carrot and swede into small bite-sized chunks. Place them on a baking tray, drizzle with some oil and sprinkle with approximately ⅔ of the spice mix and some salt and pepper.

3. Put them in the oven and cook for about 30 minutes or until they are soft. Set aside to cool slightly.

4. Thoroughly drain the tin of chickpeas and set aside.

5. In a small bowl, whisk the 2 tablespoons of olive oil and the remaining spice mix together.

6. In a large mixing bowl toss the onion, root vegetables, chickpeas and mixed lettuce together.

7. Drizzle the spiced oil into the salad and toss to coat all the salad ingredients, then serve.

Beef Stroganoff

Maggie doesn't like mushrooms. At all! So Ryan has to get creative when he wants his fix of fungi. In this recipe, he can cut them up into thin slices and hide them amongst the other ingredients. (But Maggie still finds them!)

 SERVES 4

DIETARY INFO:

- 500g beef fillet
- 25g butter
- 1 red onion, thinly sliced
- 1 teaspoon minced garlic
- 400g button mushrooms, thinly sliced
- 1 tablespoon Dijon mustard
- 250ml beef stock
- 2 heaped tablespoons soured cream or crème fraîche
- salt and pepper to taste
- finely chopped parsley to garnish

1. Cut the beef fillet into strips approximately 1cm (½ inch) wide. Over high heat, cover the base of a large pot with oil and seal the beef strips in several batches to avoid overloading the pot. Set the sealed beef aside.

2. If the pot is dry, add a little more oil and add the butter. Once it has melted, add the onions and cook while stirring for about 2 minutes. Add the garlic and continue cooking until the onions start to soften.

3. Add the mushrooms and continue to cook them until they are soft. Stir the mustard into the onions and mushrooms.

4. Pour the stock into the pot, bring it to a simmer and allow the stock to reduce by about half its volume.

5. Using a fork, whip the soured cream or crème fraîche and mix it into the sauce. Add the beef into the sauce and stir through.

6. Season with salt and pepper to taste, serve with mashed potato (see **page 24**) and garnish with the parsley.

Butternut Squash Risotto

Risotto is one of the easiest rice dishes to make once you know the proper techniques. Even Maggie's dad learned how to throw together a mean sweet potato risotto! This is a butternut squash one, but risotto is versatile and can be used with a variety of other ingredients to change up the taste.

 SERVES 4

DIETARY INFO:

- 1 small butternut squash
- 100ml cream
- 800ml chicken stock
- 1 large brown onion, finely diced
- 2 teaspoons minced garlic
- 250g Arborio rice
- 30g butter
- 1 tablespoon dry mixed Italian herbs
- salt and pepper to taste

1. Peel, deseed and chop the butternut squash into medium chunks.

2. Bring a pot of water to the boil and add the butternut squash. Cook for 7-10 minutes or until the squash is tender.

3. Using a stick blender or potato masher, puree the squash, adding the cream to help. Set aside.

4. Over high heat, bring the chicken stock to the boil then immediately turn off the heat.

5. In a separate large pot over medium heat, just cover the base with oil and lightly sweat the onions. Add the garlic and cook for a further minute.

6. Add the rice to the pot with half the butter, a pinch of pepper and the dried herbs. Stir constantly until the rice grains are very transparent.

7. Add the hot stock to the rice in roughly 100ml increments. Allow the liquid to be almost fully absorbed by the rice before adding more stock. Continue until all the stock is used.

8. Stir in the squash puree and the remaining butter. Remove the pot from the heat and allow the rice to absorb the remaining liquid for 1-2 minutes.

9. Season with salt and pepper to taste and serve immediately.

Make this recipe vegetarian and vegan-friendly by substituting the chicken stock with vegetable stock, the butter with a plant-based margarine, and the cream with soy cream.

A family of swans looking for their dinner.

Shallow Fried Crispy Cod

This recipe is perfect for making your own fish and chips at home. When we first came to the UK, we found out that Friday nights were dedicated to this deep fried treat! This floured cod is lighter than a beer battered variant and we've served ours with garlic new potatoes instead of chips.

 SERVES 2

- 400g (345g drained weight) tinned new potatoes
- 50g plain flour
- 1 teaspoon onion powder
- 1 teaspoon garlic powder
- 1 teaspoon dried dill
- 2 cod fillets (130g-150g each)
- 1 tablespoon butter
- 1 teaspoon dry mixed Italian herbs
- vegetable oil for frying
- salt and pepper to taste

1. Drain and slice the new potatoes into approximately ½ cm (¼ inch) thick.

2. In a shallow bowl mix the flour, ½ teaspoon of garlic powder, ½ teaspoon onion powder and the dried dill together. Coat the cod fillets in the flour mix and set aside.

3. Just cover the base of a pan with oil over high heat, add the potatoes and toss them for a minute. Add the butter, dried Italian herbs and the remaining onion and garlic powder and toss through.

4. Continue cooking the potatoes for about 4-5 minutes until the potatoes are starting to go brown at the edges and slightly crispy. Season to taste with salt and pepper and remove from the heat.

5. Fill a separate pan with approximately 1cm (½ inch) of oil and bring it to a high heat.

6. When the oil is hot, gently add the cod fillets to the oil. Cook each side for 3-4 minutes or until they turn golden brown. Remove from the pan and place onto kitchen towel to absorb excess oil.

7. Serve the cod with the garlic potatoes and steamed veg with tartare sauce (see **page 15**), or go traditional with a side of our homemade chips from **page 45**.

Lamb Shanks with Red Wine Sauce

We occasionally treat ourselves to lamb shanks and this is our favourite way to prepare them. It's perfect for cold days sitting by the fireplace – which also serves as our slow cooker for this recipe!

 SERVES 4 **DIETARY INFO:**

- 4 lamb shanks
- 1 brown onion, finely diced
- 1 tablespoon minced garlic
- 2 tablespoons tomato paste
- 400ml red wine
- 500ml beef stock
- 200ml tomato passata
- 2 tablespoons corn flour
- 100ml cold water

1. Preheat the oven to 180°c (350°f/gas mark 4).

2. In a large casserole dish over high heat, cover the base with oil and seal the lamb shanks in batches until brown all over.

3. Remove the lamb and drain excess fat from the dish. Add a small amount of oil to the same dish and add the onion and garlic. Cook for about 5 minutes or until the onions have softened.

4. Add the tomato paste and cook it out for a minute, then deglaze the casserole dish with the red wine. Stir in the beef stock and tomato passata.

5. Place the lamb shanks into the dish, making sure they are mostly submerged. Bring them to a simmer, then cover and put in the oven for 2 hours.

6. After the 2 hours, uncover them and continue cooking for 20-25 minutes. At this point, check if the meat is tender. If not, cover and continue cooking until it is. Ideally, the lamb should be tender and just holding onto the bone.

7. When ready, remove the lamb from the liquid. Bring the sauce to a simmer over medium heat and thicken by gradually adding the corn flour mixed with cold water if needed. Season to taste.

8. Serve the lamb shanks with mashed potato (see **page 24**) and green beans and plenty of the red wine sauce.

Beef Lasagne

Who doesn't love a good lasagne? And this is a good one! Layers of rich, beefy flavour interspersed with the creamy white sauce and topped with golden melted cheese. Just makes your mouth water thinking about it!

🍴 **SERVES 4**

- 1 medium brown onion, finely diced
- 1 teaspoon minced garlic
- 250g lean beef mince
- 1 tablespoon tomato paste
- 1 tablespoon dry mixed Italian herbs
- 1 teaspoon dried oregano
- 400g tinned chopped tomatoes
- ½ teaspoon sugar
- ½ teaspoon balsamic vinegar (optional)
- salt and pepper to taste
- 300g grated cheese
- 500g lasagne sheets

White sauce

- 40g butter
- 40g plain flour
- 500ml milk
- 2 tablespoons parmesan cheese

1. Make the white sauce by melting the butter in a medium pot over high heat. Add the flour and mix in. Stir for 4-5 minutes to cook out the flour. Don't allow it to turn brown.

2. Add half the milk to the flour and stir continuously. Once absorbed, add the remaining milk and whisk until smooth. Simmer on a low heat to thicken, season with pepper and stir in the parmesan cheese. Set aside.

3. In a pot over medium heat, add oil to cover the base and begin sweating the onions. Add the garlic and cook for a minute or two.

4. Turn the heat to high, add the beef mince to the pot and begin browning. Add the tomato paste and mix through thoroughly. Season with salt and pepper to taste and add the herbs.

5. Once the beef has browned, add the chopped tomatoes and simmer for 3-4 minutes.

6. Mix in the sugar and balsamic vinegar, simmer for a further 2-3 minutes then season to taste. Remove from the heat.

7. Preheat the oven to 190°c (375°f/gas mark 5).

8. In a deep oven-proof dish lay a very thin layer of the mince in the bottom, then place a layer of lasagne pasta sheets on top. Break the pasta sheets if needed to ensure total coverage, but try not to let them overlap or they won't cook properly.

9. Spread half of the mince evenly over the top of the pasta sheets, then add nearly half the white sauce and spread over the mince evenly. Sprinkle with cheese and cover with a layer of pasta sheets.

10. Repeat step 9 with the next layer, using the remaining mince and most of the white sauce. Finish by covering the last layer of pasta sheets with the remaining white sauce and a generous sprinkling of cheese.

11. Cover the dish with tin foil and place into the oven for 25 minutes. Finish by removing the foil and cooking for a further 10-15 minutes to allow the cheese on top to melt and slightly brown. Cut into portions and serve hot with our homemade garlic bread (see **page 51**).

Crispy Chicken Caesar Salad

We've taken some liberties with this classic salad to make it more appealing for the colder months. It has warm bacon pieces tossed through it and is topped with deliciously crunchy, panko-crumbed, shallow-fried chicken.

 SERVES 2

Caesar salad

- 2 slices of bread
- 100g bacon
- 1 cos/romaine lettuce
- 1 chicken breast
- 75g panko breadcrumbs
- 50g plain flour
- 2 eggs
- 40ml milk
- 50g shaved parmesan cheese
- 2 freshly boiled eggs
- vegetable oil for frying
- salt and pepper to taste

Caesar dressing

- 2 anchovies
- 4 tablespoons mayonnaise
- 1 teaspoon lemon juice
- 15g finely grated parmesan cheese

1. Preheat the oven to 165°c (325°f/gas mark 3). Cut the bread into approximately 1½ cm (½ inch) squares. Spread the squares on a baking tray, sprinkle with oil, salt and pepper and put into the oven for 15-20 minutes or until they are crispy.

2. Make the dressing by finely chopping the anchovies and adding them, the lemon juice and the finely grated parmesan to the mayonnaise. Mix together well.

3. Slice the bacon into chunky pieces and fry off in a small amount of oil over high heat for about 7-8 minutes or until it starts to go crispy. Place the bacon on some kitchen towel to absorb excess oil and fat. Set aside.

4. Break the lettuce leaves off the lettuce base and rinse them. Set aside to drain.

5. Slice the chicken breast in half horizontally – essentially creating two thin, flat chicken breasts. Pour the flour and breadcrumbs into two separate bowls. In a third bowl whisk the eggs and the milk together.

6. Dip each piece of chicken into the flour, then dip them into the egg mix, then finally into the breadcrumbs, giving them a good coating of each.

7. Fill a pan with approximately 1cm (½ inch) of oil and bring it to a high heat. Fry the crumbed chicken for 2-3 minutes each side or until they are a deep golden brown.

8. When ready, remove the chicken from the oil and place on kitchen towel to absorb excess oil.

9. Tear the washed lettuce leaves into bite-sized pieces and place into a mixing bowl. Add the bacon, shaved parmesan, croutons and dressing into the bowl and gently toss through the lettuce.

10. Serve the salad topped with the crumbed chicken breast and garnish with the boiled egg cut in half.

Couscous Stuffed Peppers

When your peppers are tired, they're stuffed! (We know you secretly love the puns.) This Mediterranean-inspired dish is a different way to use couscous, but you can also stuff peppers with flavoured rice.

 SERVES 4

DIETARY INFO:

- 4 large peppers with relatively flat bottoms
- ½ brown onion, finely diced
- 1 teaspoon minced garlic
- 2 tablespoons unsmoked paprika
- 1 tablespoon ground cumin
- 1 teaspoon dried oregano
- ½ teaspoon ground coriander
- ½ teaspoon cayenne pepper
- ½ teaspoon pepper
- 1 tablespoon dry mixed Italian herbs
- 1 tablespoon tomato paste
- 550ml vegetable stock
- 360g fine couscous
- 1 teaspoon margarine
- approx. 10 semi dried tomatoes, roughly chopped
- 100g sliced black olives

1. Preheat the oven to 200°c (400°f/gas mark 6).

2. Cut out the top of the peppers and use a spoon to scrape out the white pith and seeds. If needed, carefully trim the bases of the peppers to make them stable and level.

3. Place a large pot over high heat and just cover the base with oil. When hot, add the onion and begin frying, then stir in the garlic.

4. When the onion has started to soften, stir in the herbs and spices. Cook for 1-2 minutes to release the flavours. Add the tomato paste and cook for another two minutes while stirring to prevent burning.

5. Add the stock to the pot and mix well to get the flavours through it. Bring to the boil then immediately turn off the heat and add the couscous. Stir the couscous through, then place a lid on the pot and let it sit for about 5 minutes.

6. After the 5 minutes, remove the lid and stir the margarine through - this will help prevent the couscous from clumping.

7. Gently stir the semi dried tomatoes and olives through the couscous.

8. Place the peppers on a tray and fill them to the top with the couscous. Put them into the oven for about 5-10 minutes. Serve immediately when cooked.

Beef Goulash

Another recipe that we love to make on the cold winter nights on board our narrowboat is this beef goulash. It simmers away nicely on top of our coal-fueled fireplace, filling the entire boat with its rich aroma.

 SERVES 4

DIETARY INFO:

- 400g diced beef
- 3 medium onions, thinly sliced
- 1 teaspoon minced garlic
- 1 tablespoon smoked paprika
- 1 tablespoon unsmoked paprika
- 2 tablespoons tomato paste
- 1 tablespoon dry mixed Italian herbs
- 600ml beef stock
- 400g tinned chopped tomatoes
- 1 red pepper
- 1 green pepper
- 1 yellow pepper
- salt and pepper to taste
- soured cream to garnish

1. In a large pot over high heat, add enough oil to cover the base. When hot, add the diced beef and seal until all sides are nicely browned.

2. Add the onions to the beef and cook for 5 minutes until softened. Add the garlic and cook for 1-2 minutes while stirring.

3. Sprinkle both paprikas over the meat, add the tomato paste and herbs and stir through. Cook for another 1-2 minutes.

4. Add the beef stock and the chopped tomatoes, stir well and bring to a simmer. Cover with a tightly fitting lid, turn the heat down to low and cook for an hour, stirring every 10-15 minutes.

5. While the beef is cooking, cut the peppers into chunks about 3cm (1¼ inches) in size.

6. Stir the peppers into the beef after the one hour, replace the lid and continue cooking for another 30 minutes or until the beef is tender. Season to taste.

7. Serve with a small portion of rice, garnished with soured cream.

A narrowboat moored on the
Trent & Mersey Canal.

Sunrise over the Staffordshire &
Worcestershire Canal.

Sweet Potato Curry

This is one of our favourite veggie-based curries. As well as being very tasty and filling, it also uses tinned, long-life ingredients from the pantry to bulk it out and add texture and flavour.

 SERVES 4

DIETARY INFO:

- 2 medium sweet potatoes
- 2 medium brown onions
- 1 teaspoon minced garlic
- 1 teaspoon minced ginger
- 120g butter
- 3 tablespoons garam masala
- 2 tablespoons ground cumin
- 1 tablespoon ground coriander
- ½ teaspoon chilli powder (optional)
- 1 tablespoon tomato paste
- 400g (240g drained weight) tinned chickpeas
- 400g (240g drained weight) tinned lentils
- 200ml cream
- 400g tomato passata
- 400g tinned chopped tomatoes
- salt and pepper to taste

1. Preheat the oven to 190°c (375°f/gas mark 5).

2. Peel and dice sweet potato into bite-sized chunks. Spread evenly on a baking tray and place into the oven for 20-25 minutes until it is soft. Mix the spices together in a small bowl.

3. Finely dice the onions, add them to a pot over medium heat with enough oil to cover the base and begin sweating them with the garlic and ginger. Add half of the butter and melt into the onions.

4. Add the spices and tomato paste and cook for a few minutes while stirring. Add drained chickpeas and lentils to the pot. Mix in the remaining butter and cook for a further minute.

5. Stir in the cream, passata and chopped tomatoes. Simmer for about 5 minutes.

6. Remove sweet potato from the oven and add straight to the pot. Continue simmering for 3-4 minutes. Season to taste.

7. Serve hot with freshly cooked long grain rice.

Make this recipe vegan-friendly by substituting the butter with a plant-based margarine and the cream with soy cream.

Gourmet Mac & Cheese

We've given this mac and cheese recipe a slight upgrade! This one is made with three cheeses: cheddar, mozzarella and parmesan. We've also succumbed to the deliciousness of smoked pancetta...

 SERVES 2 *(OR 4 AS SIDE DISHES)*

- 180g smoked pancetta, diced
- 200g macaroni
- 30g butter
- 30g plain flour
- 300ml milk
- 50g mozzarella cheese, grated
- 50g parmesan cheese, grated
- 100g cheddar cheese, grated
- 30g fresh chives, finely chopped
- pepper to taste

1. Add a teaspoon of oil into a hot pan over high heat and begin frying off the pancetta. Cook it for 7-8 minutes or until it starts to go crisp.

2. Remove pancetta from heat and place onto kitchen towel to drain excess oil.

3. Bring a large pot of water to the boil and add a generous pinch of salt. Put the pasta in and cook for about 10 minutes or until it is *al dente*. When cooked, drain it in a colander.

4. While the pasta is cooking, melt the butter in a pot over high heat. Add the flour and mix in. Stir for 4-5 minutes to cook out the flour. Don't allow it to turn brown.

5. Add half the milk to the flour and stir continuously. Once absorbed, add the remaining milk and whisk until smooth. Simmer on a low heat to thicken.

6. Add the three cheeses and stir through until the cheeses have melted and the sauce is smooth. Season with pepper.

7. Mix the drained pasta, the chives and the pancetta into the cheese sauce and serve immediately.

Honey Soy Pork Loins

As we've mentioned previously, we love our Asian-inspired dishes. This is one that includes the delicious sweet-and-salty flavours that many people enjoy. One of the best ways to eat pork!

 SERVES 2

DIETARY INFO:

- 4 pork loin steaks
- 100ml soy sauce
- 2 tablespoons honey
- 50ml sweet chilli sauce
- 1 teaspoon minced garlic
- 1 teaspoon minced ginger
- 1 teaspoon Chinese 5 spice
- ½ teaspoon pepper
- 1 tablespoon sesame oil
- 1 spring onion, finely chopped to garnish

Stir fry vegetables

- 100g green beans, halved
- 1 yellow pepper, sliced into thin strips
- ½ red onion, finely sliced
- 2 celery stalks, finely sliced
- 2 carrots, finely sliced
- 1 red chilli, finely chopped

1. Combine the soy sauce, honey, sweet chilli sauce, garlic, ginger, Chinese 5 spice and pepper in a mixing jug and mix well.

2. Add the sesame oil to a large frying pan and bring up to a high heat. Cook the pork loin steaks in the pan for 3-4 minutes per side until well browned. Remove from the pan and set aside.

3. Next, add the stir fry vegetables to the hot pan with a little extra oil if needed. Cook for 2-3 minutes while continuously moving the veg in the pan.

4. Add about 2 tablespoons of the honey soy sauce mix to the stir fry and continue cooking for another minute, then remove the veg from the pan to the serving plates.

5. Pour the rest of the honey soy sauce into the pan and bring it to a simmer. Simmer for 2-3 minutes until the sauce coats the back of a spoon, then add the pork loin back in.

6. Glaze the loins with the sauce until they are well coated and sticky.

7. Remove from the heat and serve with the stir fry veg and a small side of rice. Garnish with the spring onions.

Spaghetti & Meatballs

One of the classics, perfect for a winter's evening and seemingly beloved by everyone from the kids to the grandparents! Making your own meatballs is easy and they taste way better than supermarket-bought ones.

 SERVES 4

Meatballs

- 500g lean beef mince
- ½ brown onion, finely diced
- 1 teaspoon minced garlic
- 1 tablespoon dry mixed Italian herbs
- 1 egg, lightly beaten

Sauce

- ½ brown onion, finely diced
- 1 teaspoon minced garlic
- 2 tablespoons tomato paste
- 1 teaspoon dried oregano
- 1 tablespoon dry mixed Italian herbs
- 400g tinned chopped tomatoes
- 100ml tomato passata
- ½ teaspoon sugar
- salt and pepper to taste
- 500g spaghetti
- 50g parmesan cheese, grated

1. Make the meatballs first by mixing the diced onion and garlic into the beef mince. Add the herbs and the egg and season with salt and pepper.

2. Fry a tiny bit of the mince mixture to check the seasoning and adjust if needed. Divide the mixture evenly into about 24 balls. A tablespoon is a good guide to the amount of mixture to use per meatball. Cover them and refrigerate until required.

3. Start the pasta sauce by sweating the onions in a pot over medium heat with enough oil to just cover the base. Add the crushed garlic and continue cooking until the onions are soft and pale gold in colour.

4. Add the tomato paste, oregano and herbs to the pot and cook for 1-2 minutes, then add the chopped tomato and tomato passata to the pot and cook for 4-5 minutes.

5. Stir in the sugar and season with salt and pepper to taste. Continue to simmer the sauce for about 10 minutes.

6. Meanwhile, bring a large pot of water to the boil and add a generous pinch of salt. Put the spaghetti in and cook for about 10 minutes or until it is *al dente*. When cooked, drain it in a colander.

7. While the spaghetti is cooking, heat a frying pan over high heat with enough oil to give a good covering over the base of the pan. Seal the meatballs in the frying pan for 4-5 minutes until all sides are nicely browned.

8. Add the sealed meatballs to the pasta sauce and cook them in the sauce for 10 minutes.

9. Serve by placing the meatballs on top of the spaghetti, ladling the sauce over the top and garnishing with the grated parmesan.

Roast Chicken Dinner

We especially love the contrast of the roasted vegetables with the fresh crispness of the coleslaw in this recipe. The honey sesame carrots lend a sweetness to the dish – and we can't forget about the good old peas!

 SERVES 2

DIETARY INFO:

- 2 chicken breasts
- 2 large potatoes
- 1 medium sweet potato
- 1 large carrot
- 2 tablespoons honey
- ½ teaspoon sesame seeds
- 120g frozen peas
- 1 teaspoon dry mixed Italian herbs
- salt and pepper to taste
- 1½ teaspoons butter

Coleslaw

- ¼ white cabbage
- ¼ red cabbage
- ½ red onion
- 1 large carrot
- 1 green apple
- 1 tablespoon lemon juice
- approx. ½ cup of mayonnaise
- salt and pepper to taste

1. Preheat the oven to 200°c (400°f/gas mark 6).

2. Cut the potatoes into quarters and cut the sweet potato into similar sized chunks. Place on a baking tray and drizzle with oil. Season with salt, pepper and half the mixed herbs. Put in the oven for about 30 minutes.

3. For the coleslaw, finely slice the cabbages and red onion. Grate the carrot and apple. Mix all together in a bowl and add the lemon juice. Add mayonnaise to your desired consistency and season with salt and pepper. Set aside in the fridge.

4. Check the potatoes and turn them to prevent burning.

5. Season the chicken breasts with salt, pepper and herbs. In a hot pan with just enough oil to cover the base, add 1 teaspoon of butter and melt it. Place the chicken in the pan with the side you plan to use for presentation facing down first. Seal all sides of the chicken until golden in colour.

6. Once sealed, place chicken in the oven on the same tray as the potatoes. Check the potatoes at the same time. Roast for about 20 minutes or until the chicken is fully cooked through.

7. Cut the carrot into rough carrot sticks and cook them for 5 minutes in boiling water. Remove the carrots, but keep the boiling water for the peas later.

8. In the same pan used to seal the chicken, heat a small amount of oil and the ½ teaspoon of butter over high heat. Add the carrots to the pan and cook for about 1 minute. Add the honey to the pan and toss. Caramelise and finish the carrots off with the sesame seeds.

9. Boil the peas for 3-4 minutes, then drain.

10. When the potatoes and chicken are ready, get the coleslaw out of the fridge and serve everything together with your favourite sauce or gravy.

Beef & Bean Chilli

To ward off the winter chill, give this tasty chilli a try! (Try saying that three times fast!) This chilli recipe is great as its own dish, but could also be used to make your own homemade nachos.

 SERVES 4

DIETARY INFO:

- 500g lean beef mince
- 400g (240g drained weight) tinned red kidney beans
- 1 large brown onion, finely diced
- 2 tablespoons tomato paste
- 400g tinned chopped tomatoes
- 250ml tomato passata
- 300g sweet corn
- 1 red pepper, finely diced
- 1 green pepper, finely diced
- salt and pepper to taste
- soured cream to serve

Seasoning mix
- 1 teaspoon chilli powder
- ¼ teaspoon cayenne pepper
- ½ teaspoon garlic powder
- ½ teaspoon onion powder
- ½ teaspoon dried oregano
- 1 tablespoon unsmoked paprika
- 1 tablespoon ground cumin

1. Mix the spices for the seasoning mix together in a small bowl and set aside. Drain the kidney beans.

2. In a large pot over high heat, add just enough oil to cover the base. When hot, add the onions and cook until they begin to soften.

3. Add the beef mince and cook while stirring until no longer pink. Make sure to break the mince up as much as possible.

4. Add the kidney beans, tomato paste and seasoning mix. Stir through and cook for 1-2 minutes.

5. Add the chopped tomato and passata and mix through. Bring to a simmer, then add the corn and peppers and season with salt and pepper to taste. Turn down to medium heat and continue to cook for about 10 minutes.

6. Serve hot with a generous amount of soured cream and steamed rice.

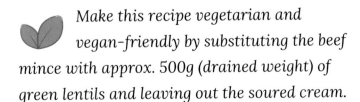 *Make this recipe vegetarian and vegan-friendly by substituting the beef mince with approx. 500g (drained weight) of green lentils and leaving out the soured cream.*

Autumn leaves in
Aston Marina.

The towpath near the village of Aston with the church spire in the distance.

Moored narrowboats blanketed in snow during a snowstorm.

Desserts

& Sweet Treats

Puff Pastry Cinnamon Rolls

Eating these crisp, puffy rolls on a cool morning while steering a narrowboat along the canals under the gloriously coloured autumn leaves is just sheer perfection. They'll disappear quickly, but it's so worth it!

 Makes 8

Dietary Info:

Cinnamon rolls

- 1 roll of puff pastry (approx. 320g)
- 3 tablespoons sugar
- 1 tablespoon ground cinnamon
- 1 tablespoon melted butter

Vanilla glaze

- 100g icing sugar
- ½ teaspoon vanilla essence
- 1-2 teaspoons milk

1. Preheat the oven to 200°c (400°f/gas mark 6).

2. Place the unrolled puff pastry on a flat surface to let it come to room temperature.

3. Mix the sugar and cinnamon together until well combined.

4. Brush the pastry with the melted butter and sprinkle the sugar mix generously over the sheet, leaving about a 2cm (1 inch) border on all sides.

5. From the long edge of the pastry, roll it into a tight scroll. Trim the ends and cut the scroll into 8 equal pieces.

6. Line a baking tray with baking paper and place the cut rolls evenly across the tray, with the spiral facing up.

7. Put into the oven for 15-20 minutes until they are golden and puffy. Remove from the oven and leave them to cool slightly.

8. While cooling, make the glaze by mixing the icing sugar and vanilla together with the milk, adding the milk gradually until the mixture is still slightly thick and holds its shape for a few seconds when drizzled.

9. Drizzle the icing over the still warm cinnamon rolls. Best eaten while warm but can be enjoyed cold.

Make this recipe vegan-friendly by using vegan puff-pastry and substituting the butter with a plant-based margarine and the milk with a plant-based milk.

Make this recipe gluten-free by using gluten-free puff pastry.

Carrot & Walnut Cake

We all know that we need five serves of vegetables a day...
Surely this means you can eat five slices of this delectable carrot cake guilt-free. Or at least that's what you can tell your friends and family as you eat it!

 SERVES 12

DIETARY INFO:

- 2 eggs
- 165g caster sugar
- 150ml vegetable oil
- 1 teaspoon vanilla essence
- 2 teaspoons ground cinnamon
- ¼ teaspoon salt
- 1 teaspoon bicarbonate of soda
- 170g self-raising flour
- 3 cups carrot, grated
- 100g walnuts, chopped into small chunks

Cream cheese icing
- 200g cream cheese
- 100g softened butter
- 300g icing sugar
- 1 teaspoon vanilla essence

1. Preheat the oven to 180°c (350°f/gas mark 4).

2. Crack the eggs into a mixing bowl and whisk briefly to combine. Mix in the sugar.

3. Gradually add the oil while continuously whisking. Once the oil is fully incorporated, add the vanilla essence, cinnamon and salt and mix in.

4. Add the bicarbonate of soda, about quarter of it at a time, ensuring it is well mixed in.

5. Stir in the flour and add the carrot and walnuts. Mix well until combined.

6. Line a round 20cm (8 inch) cake tin with baking paper. Pour the cake mix in and spread evenly with a spatula.

7. Place the cake into the oven for 40-45 minutes. When ready, remove from the oven and cool in the pan. You can check if the cake is ready by poking a wooden skewer into the centre – if it comes out clean, it's ready; if it comes out with gooey mixture on it, it's not ready!

8. When the cake is cool, prepare the icing. Bring the cream cheese to room temperature and place into a mixing bowl with the butter. Mix together until well combined and smooth.

9. Stir in the vanilla essence and sift in the icing sugar. Carefully mix the icing sugar in. If you prefer a stiffer icing, continue mixing in icing sugar until it reaches your desired consistency.

10. Remove the cake from the tray, peel off the baking paper and place onto a serving plate. Pour the icing onto the cake and spread carefully with a spatula. Allow the icing to set for at least half an hour before serving.

Sweet Scones

The classic English scone – a staple of afternoon teas around the country! Many a canal-side café offers these scrumptious treats. They're so easy to make at home that even those whose professed level of culinary skills extend to cheese sandwiches can whip these up!

 MAKES 6

DIETARY INFO:

- 225g self-raising flour
- 40g softened butter
- 1½ tablespoons sugar
- ¼ teaspoon salt
- 110ml milk + milk to brush over scones
- plain flour for kneading and cutting

These are delicious as they are, but don't be afraid to add mixed fruit or other flavourings to create your favourite scone.

 Make this recipe vegan-friendly by substituting the butter with a plant-based margarine and the milk with a plant-based milk.

1. Preheat the oven to 220°c (425°f/gas mark 7).

2. Sift the flour into a mixing bowl and rub in the butter until it has a sandy texture and all the butter is incorporated.

3. Stir in the sugar and salt. Add any extra flavouring ingredients if desired.

4. Add the milk and mix through with a fork.

5. Tip the dough out onto a floured surface and knead the dough very briefly until it is smooth. Roll it out to about 2½-3cm (1 inch) thickness.

6. Cut the dough using a round pastry cutter. Dip the cutter in flour when needed to prevent the dough from sticking to it. Place the cut scones onto a floured baking tray.

7. Brush the top of the scones with a small amount of milk and put into the oven for about 15 minutes. The scones should rise and become golden brown when they are ready.

8. Remove from the oven and leave to cool or serve warm with your choice of butter, jam, cream, or other topping!

*Melting snow
at Aston Marina.*

*Narrowboats moored along the
canal in the autumn afternoon.*

Andrea Rose
going down a lock.

Sticky Toffee Pudding

The first time we had sticky toffee pudding was while we were working as chefs in the Lakes District of the UK, before we embarked on our narrowboat adventure. It's just so decadent that Maggie *had* to learn how to make it!

 SERVES 8

DIETARY INFO:

Pudding

- 200ml hot water
- 200g soft pitted dates
- 1 teaspoon bicarbonate of soda
- 75g softened butter
- 2 tablespoons black treacle
- 50g soft dark brown sugar
- 2 eggs
- 1 teaspoon vanilla essence
- 150g plain flour
- 2 teaspoons baking powder

Toffee sauce

- 1 tablespoon black treacle
- 150g butter
- 300g soft dark brown sugar
- 200ml double cream

1. Preheat the oven to 180°c (350°f/gas mark 4).

2. Measure the hot water into a measuring jug and add the dates and bicarbonate of soda. Stir and leave for 15 minutes.

3. Put the butter, treacle and sugar into a large mixing bowl and beat them together with a wooden spoon until well combined. Beat the eggs in one at a time and add the vanilla essence.

4. Add the flour and baking powder and mix in until the mixture is smooth and thick.

5. Mash the soaked dates slightly with a fork and pour them and the liquid into the pudding mixture and combine.

6. Grease an oven-proof dish that's about 20-22cm (8-9 inches) and pour the mixture into it. Bake for 30-35 minutes.

7. While the pudding is in the oven, start the toffee sauce by heating up all the sauce ingredients except for the cream in a small pot over low heat.

8. When everything is melted, add the cream and turn up the heat. Once it starts bubbling, let it continue for 1 minute while stirring, then remove from the heat.

9. When the pudding is ready, remove it from the oven and prick it all over to help the toffee sauce seep into the pudding. Pour about a quarter of the warm sauce over it, using a spatula to get the toffee to the edges of the pudding.

10. Let the pudding sit for about half an hour to allow the sauce to become a sticky glaze. Cut into even portions and serve each portion with some of the remaining toffee sauce and vanilla ice cream.

Cupnuts

Originally named 'doughnut cupcakes,' these delicious treats were renamed when a boater friend tried to come up with a smashed together name for them – hence the 'cup' from *cupcakes* and the 'nuts' from *doughnuts*! Everyone on our YouTube channel loved it and so it's stuck!

 MAKES 12

DIETARY INFO:

Cupcake batter

- 240g plain flour
- 140g caster sugar
- 2 teaspoons baking powder
- ½ teaspoon salt
- 55g butter
- 200ml milk
- 2 eggs
- 1 teaspoon vanilla essence

Cinnamon sugar dusting

- 2 tablespoons caster sugar
- ½ teaspoon ground cinnamon
- 1 teaspoon butter for brushing

1. Preheat the oven to 180°c (350°f/gas mark 4).

2. In a mixing bowl, mix the dry ingredients for the cupcake batter together.

3. In a small pot, melt the butter and then immediately remove it from the heat. Add the milk, eggs and vanilla essence to the butter and whisk together.

4. Add the wet ingredients to the dry ingredients and whisk until just combined – don't over-mix the batter.

5. Grease a muffin tray and pour the mixture into the moulds to about ¾ full. Put the tray in the oven and bake for about 18 minutes.

6. Remove from the oven and gently run a knife around the edges of the cupcakes to remove them from the tin. Place them onto a cooling rack.

7. For the cinnamon sugar dusting, combine the sugar and cinnamon in a small bowl, making sure to thoroughly mix them. Melt the butter in a pot or microwave.

8. Use a pastry brush to brush some of the melted butter over the top of one or two of the cupcakes at a time and dip the buttered cupcakes into the cinnamon sugar mix. Repeat until all cupcakes are dusted. Best enjoyed while still warm!

Gingerbread Biscuits

The Christmas season isn't complete without this spiced cookie. Something about ginger and cinnamon brings Christmas trees, boughs of holly and brightly wrapped gifts to mind! Plus, we needed another recipe to try and use up some of that dark treacle we bought for the sticky toffee pudding!

 MAKES 40   DIETARY INFO:

- 125g butter
- 175g soft dark brown sugar
- 4 tablespoons black treacle
- 350g plain flour + extra for rolling out
- 1 teaspoon bicarbonate of soda
- 1 tablespoon ground ginger
- 1 teaspoon ground cinnamon
- 1 teaspoon ground allspice
- 1 teaspoon vanilla essence
- 1 egg, lightly beaten
- optional decorations such as writing icing and sprinkles, etc.

1. Melt the butter, sugar and treacle on medium heat and let it simmer for 2 minutes after all the ingredients have combined. Remove from the heat and let it cool for 10 minutes.

2. Add the flour, bicarbonate of soda and spices to a large mixing bowl and mix together.

3. Add the cooled sugar mixture, vanilla essence and the egg and combine until smooth.

4. Place the dough onto cling film, flatten into a rough disc to aid cooling and put into the fridge for about 1 hour.

5. Remove the dough from the fridge and preheat the oven to 190°c (375°f/gas mark 5).

6. Unwrap the dough and split it in half. Place one half on a floured surface and roll out to about 5mm (¼ inch) thickness.

7. Cut gingerbread with shaped cutters, dipping the cutters in flour when needed to prevent the dough from sticking. Re-roll dough scraps to get more biscuits out of it. Place shapes onto a lined baking tray with about 2cm (1 inch) between them and put into the oven for 8-10 minutes.

8. The gingerbread will still be slightly soft when it comes out of the oven so leave it on the baking tray for 5-10 minutes before transferring to a cooling rack.

9. Repeat with the second half of the dough. Decorate cooled biscuits if desired.

Super Triple Chocolate Brownies

We like to really load our brownies up with extra chocolate – hence the double hit of chocolate chips! If you aren't as much of a choc-a-holic sweet-tooth as Maggie, you *could* leave the chocolate chips out...

 SERVES 12

DIETARY INFO:

- 100g butter
- 200g dark chocolate, broken up
- 4 eggs
- 250g caster sugar
- 2 teaspoons vanilla essence
- 100g plain flour
- 1 teaspoon baking powder
- 2 tablespoons cocoa powder
- ¼ teaspoon salt
- 100g white chocolate chips
- 100g milk chocolate chips

1. Preheat the oven to 180°c (350°f/gas mark 4).

2. Place a small pot of water over medium heat and sit a glass mixing bowl on top of it. Make sure the water in the pot isn't touching the glass. Put the butter and the dark chocolate in the bowl and melt together, stirring often. If the water in the pot starts bubbling too rapidly, turn the temperature down until it's just simmering. Don't let any of the water get into the chocolate mix. When it's fully melted and combined, remove from the heat and leave to cool to room temperature.

3. While that's cooling, whisk the eggs, sugar and vanilla essence together until they're light and fluffy.

4. Fold the egg mixture into the cooled chocolate mixture until it's just combined.

5. Sift the flour, baking power, cocoa powder and salt into the other ingredients and fold in until just combined.

6. Add the white and milk chocolate chips and mix through.

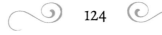

7. Line a deep 20-22cm (8-9 inch) baking tin with baking paper and pour the brownie mixture in. Even it out with a spatula, making sure the corners of the tin are also filled.

8. Place it in the oven for 25-30 minutes. When it's ready, the top should be cracked and the centre of the brownie should be just set but still fudge-like. Leave it to cool, then remove from the tin.

9. Cut into slices and serve as is, or warm them slightly in a microwave and serve with vanilla ice cream.

Apple Crumble

With the plentiful gardens that back onto the canals, sometimes we're lucky enough to find someone who has more apples from their tree than they know what to do with and are offering them free to passers-by. It's the perfect excuse to make an apple crumble!

 SERVES 4　　　　　　　**DIETARY INFO:**

Apple filling

- 5 Granny Smith apples
- 2 tablespoons soft brown sugar
- 1 teaspoon ground cinnamon

Crumble topping

- 110g rolled oats
- 85g soft brown sugar
- 85g plain flour
- 90g softened butter

 *Make this recipe vegan-friendly by substituting the butter with a plant-based margarine.*

1. Peel the apples and cut the sides off the core. Cut sides into 3mm (⅛ inch) slices.

2. Place apples into a pan over high heat. Add the sugar and cinnamon and stir over the heat for 3-4 minutes.

3. Turn the heat down to low, cover with a lid and leave to stew for about 5-7 minutes until the apples are soft but still holding together.

4. Make the crumble topping by adding the dry ingredients to a mixing bowl and mixing together. Add the butter and rub it into the dry ingredients until the mixture becomes clumpy and crumbly.

5. Spread the stewed apples evenly across the bottom of an oven-safe dish and cover with the crumble mixture, pressing the crumble down gently so that it sticks together. Sprinkle some loose crumble over the top.

6. Put the dish under the grill for 4-5 minutes until the crumble turns golden and crunchy.

7. Serve hot with vanilla ice cream.

Looking back down a flight of locks on the Shropshire Union Canal.

Mini Peach Pies

These little pies are a great way to use up end of season peaches in those early autumn months. They're also the perfect size to be able to hold in one hand while steering a narrowboat with the other!

 Makes 12

Dietary Info:

- 5-6 fresh peaches
- 2 teaspoons lemon juice
- 135g caster sugar
- 55g plain flour
- ½ teaspoon ground cinnamon
- ¼ teaspoon ground nutmeg
- 2 rolls shortcrust pastry (approx. 320g each)
- milk for brushing
- 1 tablespoon granulated sugar to top

1. Preheat the oven to 220°c (425°f/gas mark 7).

2. Peel and cut the peaches into even chunks (full slices won't fit nicely into these mini pies). Place the peaches in a bowl, add the lemon juice and stir.

3. Mix the sugar, flour, cinnamon and nutmeg together and pour over the peaches. Mix through gently.

4. Lightly grease a muffin tin and use one of the rolls of pastry to individually line the moulds of the tin.

5. Spoon the peach mixture into the pastry-lined moulds. Cut circles out of the other roll of pastry to top the pies. Crimp the edges of each pie to seal them, brush the tops with a small amount of milk, sprinkle them with granulated sugar and cut two small slits into the top of each pie to release steam.

6. Bake in the oven for 10 minutes, then turn the heat down to 180°c (350°f/gas mark 4) and continue baking for another 15-20 minutes until the crust is golden and the liquid from the pies is starting to bubble out from the slits in the tops.

7. Remove the pies from the oven and let them cool slightly before serving. Best eaten when still warm.

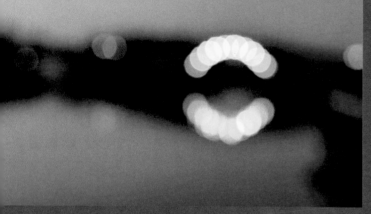

Make this recipe vegan-friendly by substituting the milk with a plant-based milk and using vegan shortcrust pastry.

Muriel's Bread & Butter Pudding

Our Patreon, Judy, sent us her mother's bread and butter pudding recipe and it's delicious! *"Mum's own home-made marmalade was always a feature of the dessert. Do use Seville orange marmalade if possible. It has a nice bite that cuts down the sweetness of the dish."*

 SERVES 8

DIETARY INFO:

- 1 loaf sliced white bread
- 250g Seville orange marmalade
- 60g butter, cut into small cubes
- 100g currants or sultanas
- 625ml milk
- 2 eggs
- 2 tablespoons sugar
- 2 teaspoons vanilla essence
- ½ teaspoon ground nutmeg

If you find you need more of the custard, the ratios are:
- 310ml milk
- 1 egg
- 1 tablespoon sugar
- 1 teaspoon vanilla essence

1. Preheat the oven to 160°c (325°f/gas mark 3).

2. Trim the crusts from the bread, then spread each slice with the marmalade.

3. Place a layer of the bread on the base of a 25cm (10 inch) dish, marmalade side up, and dot with butter. Sprinkle liberally with currants and repeat for the next layers until the dish is nearly full. Leave space at the top of the dish to allow for expansion after adding the custard mix.

4. Make the custard by lightly beating the eggs, milk, sugar and vanilla, then pour the mixture over the layers of bread. Let it sit for about 15 minutes to absorb some of the custard.

5. Sprinkle the top with nutmeg and bake for about 30 minutes until the top puffs up and the custard is set. It may take longer if you have a deeper dish with more layers. A skewer poked into the centre should come out clean when it's ready.

6. Leave the pudding to cool slightly, then cut and serve while still warm. It can also be enjoyed cold.

Judy says:

"The French onion soup followed by the bread and butter pudding have become a bit of a tradition at our place. We call them "Ugg Boot Suppers" when friends come round dressed super casual (including ugg boots of course) and we eat our food on the lounge in front of an open fire!"

You'll find the French onion soup recipe on **page 36**.

Chocolate Self-Saucing Pudding

What more could you want after a cold, wet day of cruising the canals than a rich chocolate pudding that takes barely any effort to make and warms you right through from your sodden toes to the tips of your frozen ears!

 SERVES 4

DIETARY INFO:

Pudding

- 60g butter
- 100g caster sugar
- 1 egg
- 125ml milk
- 170g self-raising flour
- 2 teaspoons cocoa powder

Sauce

- 100g soft brown sugar
- 1 tablespoon cocoa powder
- 300ml boiling water

1. Preheat the oven to 190°c (375°f/gas mark 5).

2. Cream the butter and caster sugar together until combined.

3. Lightly beat the egg and mix it into the sugar and butter, then add the milk and mix in.

4. Sift in the flour and the 2 teaspoons of cocoa powder, mixing it all together until it becomes a smooth batter. Pour the batter into individual oven-safe moulds, or into one large oven-safe dish.

5. Put the water on to boil and while waiting, mix the brown sugar and the tablespoon of cocoa powder together. Sprinkle the mix over the top of the batter.

6. Once the water has boiled, pour it over the top of the pudding(s). Ensure there is enough room for the pudding(s) to rise – ideally the batter shouldn't go past the half-way point of the moulds or dish.

7. Put the puddings in the oven for about 30 minutes if doing them individually, or 40 minutes if doing one large one. Serve hot with vanilla ice cream.

Chocolate Christmas Baubles

These baubles don't hang on your Christmas tree, but they will brighten up any Christmas party! Decorate them with the classic red, white and green of the festive season and enjoy the rich chocolate flavour!

 MAKES 25-30

DIETARY INFO:

- 300g finely crushed digestive biscuits
- 100g desiccated coconut
- 2 tablespoons cocoa powder
- 400g condensed milk

Flavour suggestions

- orange essence
- peppermint essence
- soft caramel centres
- chocolate chips
- sprinkles
- crushed nuts

Make this recipe gluten-free by using gluten-free biscuits instead.

1. Put the crushed biscuits into a mixing bowl and add the coconut and cocoa powder. Mix together.

2. Add the condensed milk and continue mixing until all the ingredients are well combined.

3. For different flavour variations, mix in other ingredients now, or leave plain for a simple chocolate flavour.

4. Form the mixture into balls of any size you like and place them onto a tray. It's easier to roll the balls if you dampen your hands slightly.

5. Place the balls into the fridge to chill for about 30 minutes, then remove and decorate them however you like, or leave them plain.

Autumn colours at the stop lock at Autherley Junction.

Aston Marina frozen over in the middle of winter.

*Trent & Mersey Canal
and towpath.*

Acknowledgements

This book wouldn't exist without all the wonderful people who watch our YouTube channel and encourage us to continue our cooking and cruising adventures. Thank you to everyone who has ever watched our videos!

Thanks to all of you who insisted we should put together a cookbook and told us you would definitely buy a copy if we did. You gave us a whole lot of confidence when we weren't sure if the effort would be worth it!

To our Patreons, you guys are amazing and your support means so much to us. Thank you for your encouragement and input into this book. It's thanks to you that this cookbook has turned out as good as it has! A lot of what we do wouldn't be possible without your generosity, so we thank you from the bottom of our hearts.

Our families and friends have been huge supporters from the beginning – thank you for believing in us and encouraging us and nagging us to get the cookbook done! Thanks also to those who graciously quality tested the food!

Thanks to Twyla for her excellent job proofreading through the book and picking up on our errors and formatting blunders. If there are any typos remaining, it's entirely Maggie's fault!

A big thank you to Stephen for helping us out with questions relating to photography and taking some lovely family portraits. And thanks for saving us from panicking when we thought we might have to retake *all* the food photos!

Thanks also to Carrie & Sue for reading through the cookbook and giving your feedback and suggestions – and for your puns!

And finally, thank you for buying this cookbook! It means so much to us. We tried hard to make this book worthy of you amazing people who support us and we hope we succeeded and that you enjoy the recipes and photography.

Thank you!

Maggie, Ryan & Pixel

Resources

If you enjoyed the recipes in this book, we have more available for free on our website that you may also like. You can visit our website at **www.narrowboatchef.com**.

We also share recipes, cooking tips and our cruising adventures aboard our narrowboat in our videos on our YouTube Channel, **Narrowboat Chef**. It's free to subscribe and watch our videos and we'd love to hear from you there! Simply search for **Narrowboat Chef** in the YouTube search bar.

If you'd like to keep up with what we're doing, connect with us on social media. You can find us on all of these platforms:

@NarrowboatChef   @NarrowboatChef

@NarrowboatQuest   Narrowboat Chef

This isn't actually the *very* first cookbook we've written; we wrote a small digital PDF cookbook called the **2020 *Lockdown Legacy Cookbook***, so if you enjoyed this one, you might like that one. It's full of inexpensive and easy meals to make during these tougher times. You can find that cookbook on our website by visiting our website and clicking 'Cookbooks' on the menu bar.

If you have any questions or comments that you'd like us to address specifically about this cookbook, you can contact us by email: **books@narrowboatchef.com**.

*Cruising our canal boat along the
Trent and Mersey Canal..*

Index

Made in the USA
Monee, IL
03 February 2021